The Cutoff

A Sequence

The Cutoff

A Sequence

Jay Rogoff

Winner of the 1994 WORD WORKS Washington Prize
The Word Works • Washington DC

Printed in the U.S.A.
Book design, typography: Joyce Mulcahy, Jude Langsam
Cover art: Lance Richbourg: *George Bell*, oil on canvas, 72" x
30", 1990. Collection of Peter John Goulandris.

Library of Congress Number: 94-061601

International Standard Book Number: 0-915380-31-5

Many thanks to the journals where some of these poems
first appeared: "The Slide" in *Chelsea*; "Long Distance" and
"Class of '80" in *Kansas Quarterly*; "In the Box," "Aesthetics,"
and "Hitting the Cutoff" in *The Kenyon Review*; "The Future"
in *Poetry Northwest*; "Everything But Everything" in *Salma-
gundi*; "Sacrifice" and "Extra Innings" in *The Sewanee Review*;
and "Over the Fence Is Out" in *Spitball: The Literary Baseball
Magazine*. "In the Box" was reprinted in *Skidmore Voices*.

The excerpt from "The Lost Children" by Randall
Jarrell, ©1969 by Mrs. Randall Jarrell, is reprinted by permis-
sion of Farrar, Straus & Giroux, Inc.

Acknowledgments

I am grateful to The MacDowell Colony, Inc., and to The Corporation of Yaddo for residencies during which I completed much of the early work on this sequence. I also thank Penny Jolly for her continued love and support as I worked on these poems, and for the tranquility and hospitality of her Cabin in the Woods. Publication of this book was assisted by a grant from the Faculty Development Committee of Skidmore College, whom I thank for their generosity.

The following books have helped me check information in this sequence and the notes to it, and given much sustenance besides: Roger Angell's *Late Innings* (New York: Simon & Schuster, 1982) and *Season Ticket* (Boston: Houghton Mifflin, 1988); *The Baseball Encyclopedia*, 8th ed. (New York: Macmillan, 1990); Paul Dickson's *The Dickson Baseball Dictionary* (New York: Facts on File, 1989); and Marc Okkonen's *Baseball Uniforms of the Twentieth Century* (New York: Sterling, 1991, rev. 1993). I am grateful for the work of these writers and researchers. Responsibility for any errors, wild pitches, or balks not accounted for in the notes rests with the author and his imagination.

"Aesthetics" is dedicated to Penny Jolly; "Why Ballplayers Spit So Much" to Karen and Ken Klotz; "Over the Fence Is Out" to friends in the Skidmore College Program at Great Meadow Correctional Facility; and "The Future" to Carolyn Sundstrom.

For My Father

Contents

Keep hitting, keep the rally alive, and you have defeated time. You remain forever young.

—Roger Angell
The Summer Game

I am tired
As a mother who's played all day, some rainy day.
I don't want to play it any more, I don't want to,
But the child keeps on playing, so I play.

—Randall Jarrell
"The Lost Children"

In the Box

A baseball knows
its calculus,
knows
    its trajectory,
      each
      inch
        from the pitcher's hand,
    when it's scheduled to curve, or tail away
    from your downtown lunge
and leave you on your ass.
You can only guess:
    no matter how you study,
      how much you've learned,

a great slider or split-
    finger,
even when you see it—red dot
    spiraling,
    white flicker—
      even when the *crack*
    starts everyone yelling,
      can devolve into a punk
        pop
        and flop
into the second baseman's mitt,
    or dribble you into a double killing.

In flight a baseball's an angel
    outshining sun or arc lights, its wings
invisible.
            Its blood-
        red
            stitches strut like seraphim;
            umpires alone have witnessed them,
                but at 90 MPH
                every stitch
                can catch
            the air some way an acoustician
            can understand—
and the ball
    sings.
            Hum,
        baby. Damned
if that ball
        don't sing. Music of the spheres. I've heard
it cauterize a hitter's soul.

Once Butch
    McCormack, down
        from the Show,
        struck out in Omaha
    and tore the water cooler from the wall. When
we'd mopped the flood, he joined me on the bench.
"I've lost it. Lost the touch,"
    a man
        shut out from a mystery
    he'd once known and could never know again.
        Swings
        buckling the hollow of your knee,
            you howl,
            sprawling in dust, wrestling those wings
                invisible
    and always in the way.

Spring

Even the grass is yearning.
You hear it in the zing
   of hot grounders
   (what Pop called daisy-cutters)—
spring
         in the grass: the stored
         sun charges
               it luminous as a Pre-Raphaelite tree,
         each blade
               injecting its juice
through my spike-blades each spring.
         I will never die.

Jays, Orioles, Cards—
birds
         build; not me. I could always feel
               the charge shoot up through grass from earth,
         feel it fill
               me like first breath—
         how could it fail?
In our B-squad's
         game chasing a liner I fell

and the shock
         of that green smell,
               of dust on my tongue
stank
               with a sulfurous sting
         and my pride hurt like a deep gash, like hell.

In this unreal southern sun
    my rhythm's screwy.
Nothing has its season—
        spring is summer or fall,
        and all
    seems a Disney
animation:
the polite fans, the motels, the tonsured green,
the oranges. I wish it would rain.

Florida's
its own world. You watch the sun rise
    out
        of the sea,
    then play a night game on the Gulf and see it set
        into the sea.
Daylight

even in March is diamond,
    merciless as Monet's summer.
        It beats down as I trudge
    to the minor-
        league complex again, my gorgeous
virgin
    67 swapped for last year's shabby 4.

Flamingos boil in jet exhaust. Any bird
    worth its salt would wing
        north
            and rip this land cyclicity
            forgot. People who believe they can't die
                seek an eternal
    spring,
        rebirth,
            the immortal
            flux of a Fountain on which a baseball
rides, in this sad state, static and absurd,
    where birds don't sing.

Out in Left Field

Crack!
    The world contracts: a spot of white
        I must stop,
    shot like light
            into the gap,
    into the dark.

Nothing! but this three-inch
    globe—wind flogs me, rushes through me—
    where's my body?—
    wind must carry
        the ball
    to me
        before I slam the wall.
            The glove
can catch
                the world: the world's cradle
                where it can nestle
            alive:
            I must save

it—I smell blood, see
    the flash
        like lights at the end
            of the clubhouse tunnel,
                unheard hearts
        pump on,
        unseen
        feet—mine?—
        I'd have sworn
                I was flying—
        pound
                hurrying
            I Got It
            I Got
It I—

                        each grassblade springing
        my feet onward and I stretch
in the utmost agony
    of reach—
                I'm an angel—
    stretch

limbs to the zodiac's far corners—
    and now, look down
    on this tiny racing man:
        and from this silent realm
        admire the form,
            the idea
                and then sweat's smell
                and blood's bang and I
gather
                        the ball
    in,

cradling in leather
    the unbroken
        egg, all
        potential,
            now held high
                in my hand
                above my head and
    rebegun
        I
jog in
through the green
world to shouts from a hundred strangers
                and let it descend
shining like Lucifer
with stitches
                to earth, to the raised mound.

North

Calgary's a jewel
and an appalling place for baseball.
        Really: we fly in from Phoenix
            or Tulsa for a spring
            series, and in the third it's flurrying
            and by the fifth snowing
like hell
and not till the blizzard starts to howl
in the seventh and we're all
crusted like Yetis will they call
the game, but we huddle in the shell
            of the clubhouse
    till traffic's
            gone, road's plowed for the bus,
and we can burst out, triumphal
    as larks.

And the park's
    electrical glitches! One night
    the P. A. kept shorting out
        so everyone's
        introductions
sounded straight from a box
            score spangled with apostrophes.
Sparks
    shot
            like fireflies
        from the speaker cones
            till *zap*—dark. A hush
            descended—then rose
            as one gasp: the aurora borealis

hung
   in a sheet
     of dazzle, greens and reds
running
   through it like a gold warp shot
     through gorgeous stuff.
On the bench, heads
bare, we watched the dark sky sing.
   Enough
baseball for one night.

Long Distance

Sound
    of her voice—huge, as if I'd put my ear
to her round belly and round
    tone, close as the clear
    air
    tonight in the star-
        struck sky of Louisville,
           close as the son of a bitch
           pitcher
        trying to kill

me with that *look out* curve
    that "didn't break"
    that broke
    my helmet, goddamn him,
because in the fifth I drove
    his fastball off the wall above the warning track—
Hey, I've
got *family*, or soon will have:
        it's not my fault his team-
        mate muffed the carom.
        And the ump didn't even eject him!
Alive

I listen to Adele, her
    play-by-play,
        what the kid's doing,
        kicking, screwing
around. She puts the receiver
        against her womb
        and I want the way I sometimes want a home
    run to say
I hear the baby stir,

but I hang up
and hope
  the ringing in my head will disappear—
God make it stop!—
  trying to fix on her
  and our Rookie of the Year.

Aesthetics

Invisible in her dark lectures
    I'd see my prof's eyes
        shine like the blues
in saintly Venetian pictures,

but it wasn't Survey where I fell—
    she wore a Yankees cap,
        halter top,
and cargo shorts, playing softball,

a faculty-family pickup game.
    Crouching behind the plate,
        "Choke the bat,"
she told her son, on the other team,

who scrunched down lower at the plate,
    held the bat at the knob,
        swung at a lob,
and popped out into his mom's mitt.

When she sprang up I watched the long
    line from behind her knee
        up her thigh
(to study its sculpture with my tongue!),

and when she batted she poked
    a soft liner past first
        and burst
out laughing as she joked

with my English prof, who said, "Some
    mother *you* are." Quick laugh.
        Then she took off
on a deep double and came home.

You can't define it and not say "beauty":
　　the pivot at second, the pitch
　　　　that can catch
the breath like Keats, Klimt, or Stravinsky.

Yet I'd seen only hard-edge lines,
　　a cool green right-angle world.
　　　　A child,
I ran from fiery disciplines,

playing ball with a boy's passion;
　　but seeing her on the field
　　　　with her child
as mother, catcher, second baseman,

feeling a pang as she held hands
　　with her husband, I saw
　　　　felicity
in Passions of the Renaissance

as well as in a double play,
　　in the curves of Samothrace
　　　　or Koufax
or her exquisitely made thigh.

Three years in dark hush I hid:
　　my heart thumped—she lectured—
　　　　our transport
when she'd say, "God, that's a gorgeous slide."

Hitting the Cutoff

Into the corner after an extra-base
    hit—may have lost
        a step but I'll nail
    the guy going home from first—
        so I wing it and watch it sail
in a gorgeous
    low parabola
on a fly to the plate and he's

safe?!
    Bo the catcher stomps
    and Skip dashes out and jumps
    up and down, his spikes dancing round the ump's,
but he's safe.
    In the dugout Skip says, "We'd
    have had him if you'd
hit Tico for the cutoff;
    I bitched to make you look good.
    Use your head—you're how old?"

30. Today. At 36
    Raphael
reached his apex,
    rising by his colors'
    dazzle and his *sfumato's*
    buzz
        to explode
    in furious
play with lights and darks,
    a hard-judging look at the weird
    shapes of the world.
    Before he could slip into his cold
    fall
    he died.
    But he had it *made.*

Pete Reiser would slam the Ebbets Field wall
    in pre-warning track
    days, black-
ing out so often while the ball bounced for a double
    it killed his wild rise
like a pistol.
        But he was crazy.

Journalists say -30- when they've hit
    The End.
Flight
    crew, prepare to crash land.
It's not right.

I leave the park
    for home and bellying Adele.
    The full
        flush of pregnancy in her
        glows like a Raphael madonna.
Candles and cake: I choke
        a slice down,
grumbling. "Hey, schmuck!"
        she says, undressing for bed. "Don't whine.
        See it in perspective."
           Eyes shut. The planet falls away,
           I dream I pass over the parabola
        of my life
        from high above
           as angels fly:
      a straight line.

Night Games

It's hard
    to come
out of, say, Pilot Field,
    that hot new stadium
in Buffalo, when you've just scored
    the winning run, and run
    downtown

to hear some decent provincial
    jazz
        and the sax
        is showy but the rhythm section cooks,
and on just your second 50 Ale
to hear at the bar the doctoral
    student from Cincinnati—who looks
    like a young Liz,
    knows
    baseball and argues
    like an angel why Pete Rose
still should make the Hall—

ask you home;
    it's hard
        year after
        year when each pitcher
    looms closer
        and looks like Bluto, and first
base appears like K-2 glimpsed in a dream
    and the Show Venus or
    Alpha Centauri,
    and the ale you've poured
        down your throat has *deepened* your thirst

until you think only the most profound suicidal
    descent
will make you whole;

                it's hard
these road nights, in love with Adele,
in love long distance even with her full
        lunar geography,
    to hear at one AM this siren, this expert
        in comparative anthropology
        sneer, "You're weird,"
        and whisper at one-thirty,
"You're a fool."
                Fidelity

on the road's a joke
        except to me,
        "The Voyaging Penelope"
        thanks to Ed. Thank God
        no one understood
so the name didn't stick.
I lug a book
                to the hotel bar
                    when Ed hangs the Do Not Disturb sign
                on our door
                    and sometimes read till dawn.

What if the moon should wander from its way,
        drop from its sphere,
            and ocean overwhelm the world?
        What if I lined
        a single to right but ran to third?
            I've known lust in the mind,
        and in Des Moines, and elsewhere;
            my pledge, my hard
        labor,
                is baseball's and Adele's: bat in hand
I battle the serpent Entropy,
        taking my place in the order.

Why Ballplayers Spit So Much

On the close-up instant
   replay super
    slo
    mo:
     nicotiana—
Red Man or Beech Nut
     chewed judiciously
   into a rich liquor
     lusciously

launched
   in an upward arc
     through the brilliant lit
   dark
      rising to apogee
       but failing
        to attain full
      escape velocity
       then falling
        in its fall
      trailing
       a tail
    a brown comet
   dark in the lit dark
wrenched

cursed
    earthward
        to the end
            of its career
                a fall
                like a black angel
                      a jet of black semen
                    with a dream
                fertile
            as air
            with a splatter
        to land
    hard
in dust.

Sacrifice

It was like a Kamikaze
        mission, one out, three
                in, tying run on third,
on the bench we're wearing our rally
                caps, inside-
        out, looking like re-

tards, yelling our heads off, when Lamarr
        skies one
                to left, Skip sends Dwayne,
                        the throw sails
                        on the fly to the catcher but pulls
him six feet foul of home, the plate is clear,

and Dwayne decides to barrel
        into him and knock
him on his tail,
                he hangs
onto the ball,
                tags
        Dwayne out, and our jaws just unlock.

Dwayne regresses
        to fetal stage. His arms clutch
his knees,
        and he screams at the trainer's touch,
                so till the doctor
                        arrives
we stand round him like Achilles
                and the Argives
                over Hector.

When Odysseus and his crew
        leave Circe's isle,
        human again but bound for hell,
they must yearn to ask him, "Why in the world did you *do*
that?" but don't dare to.
        We watch Dwayne roll
        around and want to ask, "Why in hell
        did you pull
        such a stunt? Why'd you bull
        into him and kill

the rally?" But we shut up.
        Dwayne's any of us. In his agony
        I see my years-long odyssey
                around the minors, a tour
                of battles and collisions, a Minotaur
        in Memphis, Medusa
in Phoenix, and the rapid
        dazzle
                        of late sun on the scoreboard
                and off the women's seaside summer hair. . . .
                        But hey, I would have scored.
I ain't *that* stupid.

Independence

Without
  America's
    invention there's no baseball, no paychecks,
      and we swept
    the twi-nighter, but while postgame fireworks
  sutured the skies
    I crept
to my locker and sat.
  In 1826

on the Fourth
  Adams and Jefferson,
midwives to our birth,
  both died scolding their teen-
  aged delinquent.

Another Fourth
  Gehrig
  dying
    stepped to a mike before seventy
    thousand and said, "I
consider myself the luckiest man on earth."

Watching the newsreel Pop
  cried with the crowd,
    cried two years later when Gehrig died;
      and when Gary Cooper stepped
  to bat in *Pride*
    of the Yankees, he wept
      even on the seventh screening,
even though he knew Coop
was a righty and they had to flop
    the negative
    to get him swinging
      left.

He was warming me up one day
when my junior high
    fastball
    knocked him on his tail.
        He insisted I'd screwed
          up his signs.
        By the time he died
          he was wearing my hand-me-downs.

I caromed through my teens like a pinball—
    tilt—probation and police
    blotters—God bless
America for baseball
    and lawyers, I guess.

No one's free.
    I think of Pop in my seventh-grade clothing,
how Mom's stony frugality
spared him the dignity
    of a wardrobe to die in.
Still, we gave away
        his electric razor.
    I would have used it, but after weeks of shaving
        him, when I tried to clean
        his iron
        beard from its jaws, my hand,
          as if it could catch cancer,
jerked away.

Over the Fence Is Out

In home-away-
    from-home green
        and smiles
        full of base and precious metals
they looked like they
        could kill us: ripped
from pumping iron
        and lifting crates
        of license plates,
    they popped
        the buttons off their shirts.

When we came in
the blueshirts frisking us ran
    their hands hard
        up the legs of Lamarr and Darryl
        and some of the Hispanic guys,
        who muttered and gasped,
    while Jack, who holds the record
        for RBI in Attica's
    intramural
        league but looks like Pee Wee Reese,
        escaped.

Out in the Big Yard
    the warden checked
    our sneakers, led
        the singing of the anthem and threw out
        the first ball.
    The brick wall
        in left loomed over
        us like Fenway's Green Monster,
    but rusty; so did the wall in right.
The flag atop the guard
tower barely stirred.

Ground rules:
    only one bat
        (Security, said
    the inmate ump), and over the fence was out
        (Dead
    center only 320 feet,
        and with the last Corrections
    budget cut,
buying baseballs
        out of the question).

I remember as a kid after too many drinks
curving rocks
    at windows,
        joyriding in a borrowed
    Chevy—I'd end up in a place like this!
        I'd never been so glad
    to wear grays
        and see us on the scoreboard
as "Visitors."

I grabbed the one bat
and stepped in to take my cut.
    The green, impossibly
        tall
    pitcher looked like he was doing ninety.
        His smile
           gleamed like a razor.
When I stared out
        toward the outer wall
           I saw in the tower
    three
    machine guns trained on me.

Class of '80

Don't have to read the *Alumni News* to know
    Jim's the Astros' second starter,
       Tom pitched a perfect game,
  and Rob's Seattle's leading hitter.
  I'm still here.
Even in college we flew
        more than in Triple-A,
    Rob and I helping Tom cram
    inflight for his Shakespeare final exam—
      one more D
    would drop his *cum*
  lower
       than his ERA, and he'd be history—
  so we prepped him, for the good of the team.
    Now he draws thirty
    times my salary.

Of course I haven't got a ninety-mile-
an-hour fastball,
    though as Adele reminds me,
      I'll always have the lucrative field
of Art History.
      When Ken MacKenzie of the old
        Mets complained
  he made the lowest salary
in his class at Yale,
      Casey rejoined,
  "Don't worry, you got the highest ERA."

College, we joked
  in college, prepared
  you to win at *Jeopardy*;

now it's *Trivial Pursuit.*
              To play ball?
          Hell,
no one would get it
          if I hung my *magna* in my locker;
      guys look at me weird
              if I prefer Faulkner
              on bus rides to nickel-ante poker.

Last winter I went back
and my profs could talk
of nothing but Jim's strike-
          outs and Tom's great game—
          and what a shame
I hadn't stuck

and made the majors. Hey, academics,
dear tenured intellects
      who believe
          that love
              of baseball is rooting
for the Red Sox,
                  think
of the rest of us in the sticks
          rotting
              on the brink

in the Fargos and Omahas,
dying in chrysalis,
          like Gehrig's string of back-
          ups awaiting a terrible miracle,
and damn well paying our dues
          whether or not
the goddamn *Alumni News*
              takes note.

Extra Innings

The end of this game may never come.

—Roger Angell

Playing since two, I look up
    at the blackened
midsummer sky. Three up, three down, three up,

three— Top of the thirty-second
    as we head
for the all-time pro record—

"The hell we are!" yells Ed
    in center. "Fifty
if you play a pop into an inside-

the-park." Next guy, a lefty,
    wearily lofts one shallow, and before I can think
of rapacious obstetricians and my helpless baby,

instinct
    has me under it and I'm jogging
in, Ed calling me a blankety-blank.

Too bushed to do anything
    in our half so the game enters—
good God!—the thirty-third inning.

As night cools down I hallucinate that winter's
    coming and we'll still be tied,
icicles hanging off the fielders'

caps, the diamond needing to be plowed
      every other inning, the game
spiraling on without end:

no one else can play either team
      ever again, my baby's born,
I can't help Adele, not there to choose a name,

I miss the high school graduation
      and the wedding and my first grandkid,
and I see myself falling down

dead
      diving for a liner in the top of the hundred
thousandth, spearing it to keep us tied.

Delivery

Oriole is whistling, blue jay brays,
tiger purrs, cardinal displays
alarming wings, liquid voice
recording how through hard labor
Adele has miracled our daughter,
bloody limbs, bloody face

rising like a harvest moon
tearing its way out of cloud.
My hands received her home to home
in light bright as a night ballfield.
Hoisting her, high and safe,
I relayed her to my wife.

Birds will go; beneath their wings
tigers place their prints in snow
along the winding, dwindling path
beyond a Flemish angel's window,
far from summer's songs of Ruth,
choiring with a manager's lungs.

Pop

Issue of my miraculous news:
we win a close one, and in the clubhouse
    a cake—
pink icing roses,
pink icing bats and gloves
    and

```
*  *  *  *  *  *  *  *
*   Congratulations   *
*         POP         *
*  *  *  *  *  *  *  *
```

       Pop?
    Hell of a nick-
          name—
          P. A.'d pregame
          with the starting lineup.
       Even fans
     in the grandstand
          who don't care who the hell I am
          shouting, "Get a hit, Pop!"

Pop!
    Hell, I'm 30, I can rip a curve pretty fair;
        you'd think I was a goddamn *grand*dad
to hear Tico at shortstop
yell, "Yo, Pop!"—
      the kid
      can't buy a legal beer!

Once when Pop
      took me to the Stadium to see
      the Yanks whomp Kansas City,
the old A's, around the fifth he stood up
        and pointed out
           to the bullpen. Satchel Paige
        was throwing heat.
      He was over sixty,
          an age

lots of folks don't reach alive.
   (KC had no gate attraction;
   Satch was two months shy of a big league pension.)
      In the eighth, the game long lost,
when all in gold he jangled in to relieve,
      shooting strikes past
         Maris and Mantle,
         scratched only by a bloop single,

Pop said, "See? You're never
   too old."
I watched Pop not long after
shiver
      in his small railed
         bed,
            hooked to tubes, a newborn
in an incubator.
            I think of Adele, of diapers on a line,
         of Ruth's perfect, fragile head.
Will I *ever*
   get called?
            Champagne
   corks pop. Coiled,

then sprung from the tunnel you discover
you're on a roller
      coaster. *Father.*
You're never
      too young, either.

The Slide

Level
    as the field
    may be, from second to third, third
to home is all
uphill.
       Yet how often
       you must go *down*
    in the dirt and slide,
as if descent were arrival.

Ruth arriving fell
    into my astonished hands,
    though journeying from the wetlands
within her small hill
uphill
    to my waiting finger-stones,

her head-
    first run through the nar-
       row channel, through the delta
    to safety,
a tough slide
    to the sea of open air.

You always want it to cease
    being tough, the channel
less treacherous
until you realize
    you'd then head downhill
anticipating the ax, your release.

Ruth's release into the relief

of sweat tinged
    with air,
air tanged
      with grass, had to hurt
     as this latest slide pained her aging father,
      late,
tagged
     at the plate.
       Even standing
after dusting it off,
       I felt the descending
   body, harangued
      by blood, relieved by dirt.

September 1

Like Christmas; my gift's
    the lump of coal.
Skip locks his office and sits
    with me till

the guys leave. "They want kids.
    Hell, in sixth place
they don't care squat for heads;
    a new face

to bring 'em in." They've called
    up Dwayne and Darryl,
a nineteen-year-old, wild,
    just-out-of-high school

pitcher, and a bunch
    more, including
a guy Skip only had pinch-
    hitting!

We go for a beer and sit
    in one of the dives
on an uncertain street
    where bars like caves

can swallow you whole. "It ain't
    like Nam, or the world
ending; it's ball. You got
    your little girl,

and Adele's the sanest woman
    I know." God
knows he's right, but tears swim in.
    Some explode

on the beer-burnished bar.
    In the dark, lipstick
glows, searching for
    a trick.

The Future

Remember that mountain?
At season's end we chose one known
for views in every direction
        and started up.
Soon
strain
        stained our foreheads. I wrung
    my cap,
        like a tree you shook out long
hair. It started to rain

torrents. Ground
    gave beneath,
we slipped a step for each two gained,
    our breath
        labored, we clutched
        at trees, roots, and when you touched
my face your hand
            exhaled
    a death-
            ly cold.

Suddenly
    emerging
at the peak, eternity
spread before us, we saw
    nothing:
        fog let
        us move ten feet
    along
    rock verging
        on a sheer
        drop, somewhere.

We clung
    cold
        as we were
        to each other,
   held
on in the sting
      of weather—

like being dead,
hand in hand, shades wed,
rehearsing for the journeying ahead.

Harvest Moonrise

The moon rose out of a cloud in centerfield, gold
   face full
      above the ghostly 434—
      nothing "minor"
   about Syracuse's centerfield wall,
         deeper than any of the NL's,
            painted blue like the summer twilight sky's
              deep amethyst
     and Adele's
       eyes; and like the face
of a big ugly child
          arose
                a gold moon waiting to be kissed.

During BP as I'd jogged the warning
   track,
      past me swooped
        a great blue heron, a refugee from Onondaga's
   burning lake—
      Dow's dump—
lumbering
       like an ibis
       or a dinosaur.
    I watched it flap
       about the outfield, clear
       the fence and disappear.

In the ninth, the bases
full,
the full
moon rose
out of the cloud in centerfield
and I recalled
laying my head against round Adele
and the baby's nine-month bed;
and now the round red
ugly kid-mug winked like the Babe: "Hiya, kid."

And I *saw*
the rotation
on the pitch
and *heard* each stitch
say,
"I'm a four-seamed hard one."

I tried to drive
it out to that red harvest smile, and the crack
was no crack I'd ever heard, no bone, no rifle
putting down a buck;
I'd dreamt of it like the dive
that turns the diver sheer arc
or the chisel's slam that sprays marble
leaving the thigh of a god.
As I rounded first a handful
cheered
and jogging to second
I smiled at the ignorant
whitening
moon climbing against the quickening
dark.

Everything But Everything

When Elizabeth at last accepts Darcy
  you've expected it so long
it's a surprise.
    You know everything
    except everything,
        as you know the copper beech
        will stretch
out in the sky but can't surmise
    each

gnarl, limb, or leaf. When I stand
out in left
        and we're far ahead,
      and Gary's got command
        of his slider, I see the game's grid
        laid
      over the ground,

over the green variables
of our skills
and lynx-alertness of our souls,
    how our beginning
        spins
    out of this three-out, nine-inning
      circumference
          we march into and then must wander
          through, the way a character
        in a romance doesn't know he's in a romance
        but takes ogres and dragons
as they come, as Dante sinks through circles
    believing
his goal's
      Beatrice

                    while obedient to the thorned structure
            of the cosmos;

so the frame of the world depends
        on the horizontal dive at third,
                on Jack's leap in right, his glove just clear
of the fence
                to pluck the ball from air,
                        and on the torque of wrist
that sends
                                it sailing, each a local
                                miracle
                without which this goodly structured
                        frame would not exist.

We sail into the unknown, you and I—
        have we sailed too far?
                To navigate a marriage through the minors
                        is like voyaging
into the old North Atlantic: *Here There Bee*
        Monsters,
                        and we must guess
                                the world is round, must suppose
                we'll keep striking shores
                                where we can trade
                                in gold
        and take on fresh water,
        and as far
as what befalls you and me,
we watch the coastline and assume we know
                everything but everything.

Fall

Across the infield grass
    that's endured the heat of summer
    a red leaf tilts. Another. Two more.
I pace the field, returning too late as to a now-strange house
        where I'd lived half
        my life—
            new-painted, added-onto—an exile.
        It might as well
be ice,

a field of undulating ice
    lit
    by the white
        moon.
The farmer who made the dirt breathe can only gaze,
        beer in hand.
    Down
    I come like glistering Phaeton!
Cut.

The agony of Masaccio's *Expulsion*: in braille
    fingers, Adam buries
    his face;
        Eve grips breast
and mons, shrieking. A wail
        like a holocaust.
The world is hell.

Kinder,
    Milton bids them towel their tears and set out
        holding hands,
a great adventure;
    still in Eden, we watch them depart:
        we're their parents:
            Be careful!
        Your hand, Adele.

Brown
    Padres shake
        their heads,
            Cardinals
    burn black smoke.
            Angels
who blind
        wag flaming swords
            while high above stern Astros
frown.

It grows colder.
    I once said no one's free;
        now, winning release,
            should I put into port,
            abort
    this odyssey?
        Or some newer place,
        east of Enid, Oklahoma, west of the sunrise—
            some new ball-
park light-years further
        from Paradise?
        On clear nights moon striking the fields of ice
            will dazzle waves of a frozen
            ocean;
        down into dawn I'll listen for the snow's
            fall,
                my father beneath;
Ruth needs a father,
                skating above.
    We all need a home. Free agency.
    Choose.

Limbo

Things are a lot more like the way
they are now than they ever were.

—Yogi Berra

Flying
    east years ago to my
first spring camp, out over the wing
    I saw a city flaming in the sky.
    Sunset lit the clouds
        and made them marble, steel, and glass,
        and in those buildings crowds
had stopped work and were listening
        to the Series
        on gold radios.

Homer, Euripides, Aristotle,
    I know how they feel
        on their Dantean clouded-over picnic.
    Good mates, epic and philosophic
    schmooze, putting the occasional
half-hearted futile
        move on Sappho—a full
            life, with no
final
        joy.

Washed up onshore I return,
a thirty-year-old smiling bubblegum man.

Triple-
A is Limbo—not the lower bushes' deep circle
    where ancient sweat yellows
    your uniform and prairie dogs colonize
        left field, but still
            it's Omaha, or Syracuse, New York.
    You see, Adele,
        still an adolescent schmuck,
            goggles trained on the Bigs
            while struggling up the crags
    of Pisgah, dreaming of the call.
    Why have you put up with all

this?—nine apartments in seven years,
    every draft or trade
    blowing us like tumbleweed
        to towns that had as team mascot
            a giant lizard
and for a bus station, when drivers
        wouldn't forget,
            a phone booth in the desert.

And visiting you punching registers
    or waitressing,
in spare corners—
            until some apoplectic redneck boss would scowl
    you back to work—reminiscing
            about college,
            yesterday, an age
    ago, I'd hate myself for this hell
I've dragged you through, circling
        the open road's tightening wheel
            and if we ever got anywhere anyhow
            it'd *still* be Wichita

                    until
                               you'd put a finger to my lip
                               sneak me
                               a cup of coffee
                               and I'd leave a dollar tip.

Above that burning
        city, consumed with pennant fever,
            I had a vision
                my love,
            teammates angelic in satin
    glittering
            beneath the home lights, diamond,
                        where somehow the game
                            even with its limitless
                                innate uncertainties became a house,
                            the hearth warm,
    sheltering
        each player, each lover
                safe,
                home.

Notes for *The Cutoff*

The Cutoff takes place at the highest level of minor league baseball, AAA ("Triple A"), one step below the major leagues. The sequence takes some mild liberties with baseball history and baseball fact; for example, the cities mentioned do not actually field teams in the same league. Other alterations are mentioned in some of the notes below.

In the Box. The *slider*, a hard-thrown pitch that curves slightly and breaks sharply downward, and the *split-finger*, a fastball that also breaks downward, are both powerful weapons against batters. The best hitters can identify a pitch's spin, or rotation, soon after it leaves the pitcher's hand, by picking up the idiosyncratic pattern of the ball's red stitches and white leather. A hard slider appears to have a *red dot*, created by the spiraling stitches. A weaker slider, which might not break as suddenly and therefore be easier to hit, shows a *white flicker*.

Spring. During spring training, teams often play two exhibition games at the same time against two different teams by dividing the roster into an A-squad, with many of the team's regulars and top prospects, and a *B-squad*, considered the less talented team.

A minor leaguer trying to earn a major league job generally wears a high uniform number. If demoted from the parent club to the AAA-level team, he would lose his new major league uniform, his *67 swapped for last year's shabby 4*, a recycled minor league jersey.

Long Distance. The *warning track*, a wide, grassless path that rings the outfield, alerts outfielders pursuing the ball that they are approaching the fence.

Hitting the Cutoff. *The cutoff* is a key fielding play that occurs when the opposition gets a hit with runners on base. The outfielder must hit the cutoff man—that is, throw to a pre-designated infielder—who then must decide in a split second whether he can throw a runner out at home or whether he should prevent another runner or the batter from advancing.

"Pistol" Pete Reiser played outfield for the Brooklyn Dodgers during the 1940s. His frequent crashes into outfield walls shortened his career and led to the innovation of the *warning track*.

Night Games. *Pete Rose*, major league baseball's all-time record-holder in hits, times at bat, and games played, was banned from baseball in 1989 for betting on baseball games and is therefore ineligible for election to baseball's *Hall of Fame*.

Sacrifice. In a *sacrifice* play, the batter makes an out in order to advance or score a runner. On a sacrifice fly, the runner on third comes home after a fielder has caught a fly ball.

On the bench, teams attempting late-inning comebacks sometimes superstitiously wear their caps backwards, inside-out, or in some other eccentric fashion, turning them into *rally caps* to encourage hitting and scoring.

Independence. A *twi-nighter*, or twilight-night doubleheader, is two games played on the same evening, beginning at 5 or 6 PM. Now rare in the major leagues, twi-nighters survive in the minors.

Lou Gehrig, the New York Yankees' great first baseman of the 1920s and 1930s, played fourteen years without missing a game until stricken with amyotrophic lateral sclerosis, which killed him just before his thirty-eighth birthday. Right-handed *Gary Cooper* played the left-handed Gehrig in the 1942 film *Pride of the Yankees*.

Over the Fence Is Out. *Pee Wee Reese*, the Brooklyn Dodgers' shortstop in the 1940s and 1950s, was one of the white teammates who most assisted Jackie Robinson's racial integration of baseball in 1947. The *Green Monster* is the 37-foot high left field fence in Boston's Fenway Park.

Class of '80. *ERA*, Earned Run Average, indicates how many runs a pitcher's opponents score against him per nine innings pitched (the length of a complete game). A lower ERA therefore means a more effective pitcher.

Casey Stengel managed both the powerful New York Yankee teams of the 1950s and the miserable New York Mets in the early 1960s. *Ken MacKenzie* was the only pitcher with a winning record on Stengel's famous 1962 Mets, who lost 120 games.

Because Lou Gehrig played 2,130 consecutive games for the Yankees, his *string of backups* at first base saw little action, barring a *terrible miracle* (see note for "Independence").

Pop. *Satchel Paige*, who pitched in the Negro Leagues in his prime and then in the American League during his mid-40s, was actually 59 in 1965 when Kansas City signed him. He pitched in one game, starting (not relieving) against the Boston Red Sox (not the Yankees), going three innings, and allowing no runs and one hit.

September 1. On *September 1*, major league teams can expand their rosters from 25 to 40 players for the last month of the season, and *call up* players from the minor leagues.

Harvest Moonrise. A *four-seamed* fastball travels faster and with more of a "hop" than a two-seamed fastball, which is gripped differently.

Limbo. In the 1940s, the Brooklyn Dodgers and Boston Braves experimented with *satin* uniforms to improve players' visibility to fans at night games.

About the Author

Jay Rogoff was born in New York City and educated at the
University of
Pennsylvania and
Syracuse Univer-
sity. He has taught
writing and
literature at
Syracuse Univer-
sity and LeMoyne
College. He
currently works for
Skidmore College
as an administrator and teacher in their Inmate Higher
Education Program. He has won numerous prizes including
an Academy of American Poets Award, the Delmore
Schwartz Poetry Prize, and the Poetry Society of America's
John Masefield Memorial Award. He has been a fellow at
MacDowell and Yaddo. His work has been published in such
magazines as *The Georgia Review*, *The Hudson Review*, *The
Kenyon Review*, *Mademoiselle*, *The New Republic*, *The Paris
Review*, *The Quarterly*, and *The Yale Review*. He is currently
working on a novel and recently completed *Venera*, a sonnet
sequence inspired by Jan van Eyck's Ghent Altarpiece. Since
childhood, except for brief flirtations with the Baltimore
Orioles and rock'n'roll, he has been devoted to the New York
Yankees. *The Cutoff* is his first published book.

About the Artist

Lance Richbourg, born in 1938, studied art at UCLA. He
teaches art at St. Michael's College in Colchester, Vermont.
Since 1976, he has been showing his paintings at the O. K.
Harris Gallery in New York City. His father, also named
Lance Richbourg, played outfield in the major leagues,
mostly with the Boston Braves in the 1920s and 1930s.

The Cutoff is the winner of the 1994 Word Works Washington Prize. Jay Rogoff's manuscript was selected from 420 manuscripts submitted by American poets.

First Readers:
Jamie Brown
Michael Davis
Elizabeth Follin-Jones
Reuben Jackson
Karen Medailleu
Rod Wilson

Second Readers:
Yana Djin
Howard Gofreed
Barbara Goldberg
Mary Hilton

Final Judges:
Karren L. Alenier
J. H. Beall
Robert Sargent
Ron Wilson
Anonymous—Contest Director

Other Books in the WORD WORKS Series:

* Washington Prize winners
**Capital Collection

WORD WORKS Anthologies

About WORD WORKS

The WORD WORKS, a nonprofit literary organization, publishes contemporary poetry in collector's editions. Since 1981, the organization has sponsored the Washington Prize, an award of $1,000 to a living American poet. Each summer Word Works presents free poetry programs at the Joaquin Miller Cabin in Washington, DC's Rock Creek Park. Annually two high school students debut at the Miller Cabin Series as winners of the Young Poets Competition.

Since Word Works was founded in 1974, programs have included "In the Shadow of the Capitol," a symposium and archival project on the African-American intellectual community in segregated Washington, DC; the Gunston Art Center Poetry Series (including Ai, Carolyn Forché, Stanley Kunitz, Linda Pastan, among others); the Poet-Editor panel discussions at the Bethesda Writer's Center (including John Hollander, Maurice English, Anthony Hecht, Josephine Jacobsen, among others); Poet's Jam, a multi-arts program series featuring poetry in performance and many other events and educational programs such as a poetry workshop at the Center for Creative Non-Violence (CCNV) shelter.

Past grants have been awarded by the National Endowment for the Arts, the National Endowment for the Humanities, the DC Commission for Arts and Humanities, the Witter Bynner Foundation, and others, including many generous private patrons.

Word Works is a member of the Poetry Committee of the Greater Washington, DC, Area, which is centered at the Folger Shakespeare Library. The WORD WORKS has established an archive of artistic and administrative materials in the Washington Writing Archive, housed in the George Washington University Gelman Library.

Please enclose a self-addressed, stamped envelope with all inquiries.